First World War
and Army of Occupation
War Diary
France, Belgium and Germany

1 DIVISION
Divisional Troops
216 Machine Gun Company
17 March 1917 - 28 February 1918

WO95/1256/2

The Naval & Military Press Ltd
www.nmarchive.com
Published in association with The National Archives

Published by

The Naval & Military Press Ltd

Unit 10 Ridgewood Industrial Park,

Uckfield, East Sussex,

TN22 5QE England

Tel: +44 (0) 1825 749494

www.naval-military-press.com

www.nmarchive.com

This diary has been reprinted in facsimile from the original. Any imperfections are inevitably reproduced and the quality may fall short of modern type and cartographic standards.

© Crown Copyright
Images reproduced by permission of The National Archives, London, England, 2015.

Contents

Document type	Place/Title	Date From	Date To
Heading	WO95/1256/2 216 Machine Gun Co Mar 17-Feb 18		
Heading	1st Division Divisional Troops 216th IT. M.G. Coy. March 1917 To Feb 1918		
War Diary	Le Havre	17/03/1917	21/03/1917
War Diary	Proyart	22/03/1917	16/04/1917
War Diary	Mericourt-Sur-Somme	17/04/1917	17/04/1917
War Diary	Mericourt	18/04/1917	20/04/1917
War Diary	Mericourt-Sur Somme	21/04/1917	21/04/1917
War Diary	Mericourt	22/04/1917	25/04/1917
War Diary	Mericourt Sur Somme.	26/04/1917	26/04/1917
War Diary	Mericourt	27/04/1917	30/04/1917
War Diary	Mericourt Sur Somme	01/05/1917	01/05/1917
War Diary	Mericourt	02/05/1917	07/05/1917
War Diary	Mericourt-Sur-Somme	08/05/1917	08/05/1917
War Diary	Mericourt	09/05/1917	16/05/1917
War Diary	Mericourt-Sur-Somme	17/05/1917	17/05/1917
War Diary	Mericourt	18/05/1917	18/05/1917
War Diary	Mericourt-Villers Bretonneux	19/05/1917	19/05/1917
War Diary	Villers-Bretonneux	20/05/1917	26/05/1917
War Diary	Moving	27/05/1917	27/05/1917
War Diary	Berthen	28/05/1917	28/05/1917
War Diary	Berthen-Heksken	29/05/1917	29/05/1917
War Diary	Westoutre	30/05/1917	11/06/1917
War Diary	Westoutre-Wallon Capel Area	12/06/1917	12/06/1917
War Diary	Hazebrouck and Wallin Capel area.	13/06/1917	14/06/1917
War Diary	Wormhoudt	15/06/1917	15/06/1917
War Diary	Malo-Les-Bains	16/06/1917	16/06/1917
War Diary	Coxyde-Les-Bains	17/06/1917	18/06/1917
War Diary	Nieuport Bains. Trenches	19/06/1917	28/06/1917
War Diary	Nieuport Bains	29/06/1917	30/06/1917
War Diary	Trenches. Nieuport Bains	01/09/1917	01/09/1917
War Diary	Nieuport Bains	02/07/1917	17/07/1917
War Diary	Coxyde	18/07/1917	18/07/1917
War Diary	St. Pol	19/07/1917	19/07/1917
War Diary	Le Clipon Camp	20/07/1917	22/10/1917
War Diary	Erkelsbrugge	23/10/1917	25/10/1917
War Diary	Houtkerque Area	26/10/1917	06/11/1917
War Diary	Dirty Bucket Camp	07/11/1917	24/11/1917
War Diary	Tunnelling Camp Ref Sheet 27 1/40,000	25/11/1917	25/11/1917
War Diary	Tunnelling Camp	26/11/1917	27/11/1917
War Diary	Sheet 27 1/40,000 F16a	28/11/1917	28/11/1917
War Diary	Proherz Area	29/11/1917	30/11/1917
War Diary	Proherz Area Sheet 27 1/40,000 F16a.	01/12/1917	01/12/1917
War Diary	Proherz Area	02/12/1917	03/12/1917
War Diary	Woesten Area	04/12/1917	05/12/1917
War Diary	Marie Farm Sheet 20 1/40,000	06/12/1917	06/12/1917
War Diary	Marie Farm	07/12/1917	21/12/1917
War Diary	Ref. Sheet Bixschoote 20 S. W H 1/10,000	21/12/1917	21/12/1917
War Diary	Marie Farm	22/12/1917	31/12/1917

Heading	1st Division War Diaries 216th M.G. Corps forms Part of M.G. BN. from 1st January to 28 February 1918		
War Diary	Marie Farm T 27 a 7.5	01/01/1918	01/01/1918
War Diary	Ref. Sheet 20 1/40,000	02/01/1918	02/01/1918
War Diary	Marie Farm	03/01/1918	31/01/1918
War Diary	Marie Fm.	01/02/1918	06/02/1918
War Diary	Sieze Camp B. 27 a 5.1 (Sheet 58 N,W)	07/02/1918	07/02/1918
War Diary	Morteld Je Est	08/02/1918	08/02/1918
War Diary	Ref. Map St Julian Morteldje Est C. 15. A 90.50	08/02/1918	08/02/1918
War Diary	Turco. Fm. Ref Map St Julian 1/100000 C. 15. C 20.25	09/02/1918	09/02/1918
War Diary	Turco Fm	10/02/1918	10/02/1918
War Diary	Canal. BK C. 25.a. 50-80	11/02/1918	17/02/1918
War Diary	Canal Bank	18/02/1918	28/02/1918

WO 95/1256/2

216 Machine Gun Co

Mar 17 – Feb 18

1st Division

Divisional Troops

216th. M. G. Coy.

MARCH, ~~December 1917~~ 1917
TO FEB 1918

WAR DIARY
or
INTELLIGENCE SUMMARY. (O.T.)
(Erase heading not required.)

No. 216 Machine Gun Coy. Army Form C. 2118.

Place	Date	Hour	Summary of Events and Information	Remarks and references to Appendices
LE HAVRE	17/3/17	12.30 a.m.	Two Sections of the Company and H.Q. with the nucleus of C. Section disembarked and marched to Shed R to await the remainder of the Company. They came over in the "QUEEN ALEXANDRA".	IQO
		2.30 p.m.	The "MANCHESTER IMPORTER" with its Transport and remaining Section arrived. Disembarkery was carried on immediately and took till dark. The Company then marched to No 2 Rest Camp arriving about 11.0 p.m. The strength of the Coy. is 10 Officers, 143 O.R. 52 animals, 2 R.E 84 O.R. and 2 animals attd. The weather kept very fine.	
LE HAVRE	18/3/17		The Company was inspected for deficiencies in clothing equipment etc. Immediately made up. The weather was still very summery and fine	IQO.
LE HAVRE	19/3/17		All deficiencies were completed. The G.S. Wagon arrived with its drivers. Four mules were unprovided & held up the 2 mules we were short. The nearial remedies had not yet arrived. The day was spent in cleaning up the weather was fine during the day, developing into a strong wind and heavy rain at night.	IQO.
LE HAVRE	20/3/17		The Company was largely employed on camp fatigues. the Gun Co. was thoroughly cleaned the animals repicketted, 2nd Lieut SYLVESTER organised the morning but returned to hospital. The weather had cleared during the morning & strong winds came on which lasted till about 3 p.m.	IQO
LE HAVRE	21/3/17		The day was spent by the Company preparing to move. Grain was carried to be ready to entrain at 3.0 p.m., afterwards altered to 11.30 a.m. and entrained at 2nd. The Company paraded at 11.30 p.m. Via No 1. Entraining Point, GARE DES MARCHANDISES, HAVRE. The weather was stormy during the day, but fine at night.	IQO

Army Form C. 2118.

WAR DIARY
or
INTELLIGENCE SUMMARY.
(Erase heading not required.)

Instructions regarding War Diaries and Intelligence Summaries are contained in F.S. Regs., Part II. and the Staff Manual respectively. Title pages will be prepared in manuscript.

Place	Date	Hour	Summary of Events and Information	Remarks and references to Appendices
PROYART	22.3.17	1.30 a.m	The Company entrained at HAVRE. Some difficulty was experienced in entraining the mules. No R.T.O. was present until 10 min. before the train moved off. The train started. We had 3 days rations on board.	
		4.20 a.m	There was a halt of breakfast for half an hour at MONTEROLY BUCHY. This was not sufficient time allowed. Ration for the day was moderate. All Officers had breakfast have been better to have saved their first to starting hall.	
		9.30 a.m	The train arrived at LA FRAQUE where we detrained. No official instructions had been given as to the place when or were to detrain. (1) The probable time of arrival. (2) The location to which we were proceeding.	III.B
		8.0 p.m	We were met at the station by approx. ¾ of an Officer, who told us we were detrained at that division. The majority of the Company were sent on to the Reinforcement Camp near PROYART, the remainder following when the clothing was collected, arriving about 11.30 p.m. There was over during the greater part of the journey, & it was fine at night.	
PROYART	23.3.17	9.30 p.m	The day was spent in cleaning equipment and sorting clothes. The C.Q.M.S. went into Amiens with Lieut. Col. O.C. and the various branches of S. Weather fine and rather night.	III.B
PROYART	24.3.17		The day was spent in cleaning. Great difficulty was experienced in getting the limbers clean owing to the scarcity of water. The cleaning of the S.A.A. of the 2/2.0 the weather was fine and sunny. A cold wind about forenoon A.F.	III.B
PROYART	25.3.17		Summer time started. The arrival of the Transport was interfered with & reported in 2. Two cases of German measles were found in the Company. The day was passed in ordinary duties. It rained all day.	III.B
PROYART	26.3.17		The Company was put in relation to weaken. A Company Canteen was consequently started. The day was spent in ordinary duties. There were about showers of rain and hail.	III.B

WAR DIARY
or
INTELLIGENCE SUMMARY.
(Erase heading not required.)

Army Form C. 2118.

Place	Date	Hour	Summary of Events and Information	Remarks and references to Appendices
PROYART	27.3.17		The day was spent in ordinary parades. The weather was still stormy. The camp was fenced round its entire isolation. The Coy was medically inspected.	200
PROYART	28.3.17		The morning was spent in cleaning up. The Coy was medically inspected. The General Box respirators were issued and fitted. Major General E.P. STRICKLAND, C.B. CMG, D.S.O. inspected the 1st Divn. Coy and complemented them on their smart turn out, and was especially pleased with the Transport. There was a sharp frost in the morning. The day was fine but cloudy at times.	207
PROYART	29.3.17		The morning was spent in ordinary parades. The box respirators were tested in lachrymatory gas during the afternoon. The weather was rainy.	270
PROYART	30.3.17		The day was spent in ordinary parades. A new system of latrines was started. The day was showery.	200
PROYART	31.3.17		The morning was spent in ordinary parades. In the afternoon, inter-sectional football matches were arranged. The day was fine, but stormy towards evening.	236

J.G. Down
Capt.
O.C. 2/10 Middx Coy.

WAR DIARY
or
INTELLIGENCE SUMMARY

(Erase heading not required.)

Army Form C.2118.

216 M.G. Coy

Vol 2

Instructions regarding War Diaries and Intelligence Summaries are contained in F.S. Regs., Part II. and the Staff Manual respectively. Title pages will be prepared in manuscript.

Place	Date	Hour	Summary of Events and Information	Remarks and references to Appendices
ROYART	1-4-17		A Church Service, C. of E., voluntary, to other denominations was held in the morning. In the evening, an informal concert was held. Very wet & cold.	A92
ROYART	2-4-17		The day was passed with normal brigade fatigues. Very rainy all day, owing to snow in the evening.	DXO
ROYART	3-4-17		Normal fatigues were carried on. The weather was fine but cold. Limbers were too wet to allow out-door work teams etc. ground.	DXO
ROYART	4-4-17		Normal fatigues were carried out. The day was stormy, ending in wet snow.	DXO
ROYART	5-4-17		The weather was very fine. Opportunity was taken by the Company to get on in Emplacement and trench tagging. The Company was placed out of quarantine.	DXO
ROYART	6-4-17		The morning was engaged in digging. The Company had men practically been taught & had the entrenching tool instruction in the A.P. Training Centre had you-day useful into the Company. Goods head. The Company moved to Bois Bleu station in the afternoon.	DXO
ROYART	7-4-17		The morning was devoted in normal parades. In the afternoon football was arranged and a concert in the evening. The remainder of the men had their own exhibitors period and control. The day was stormy.	DXO
ROYART	8-4-17		Services for C. of E. were held. No other denomination was available. A mobile aeroplane came over in the afternoon. The day was warm and sunny.	DXO
ROYART	9-4-17		Normal parades continued. Weather very ordinary, stormy.	DXO

Army Form C. 2118.

WAR DIARY
or
INTELLIGENCE SUMMARY.
(Erase heading not required.)

Instructions regarding War Diaries and Intelligence Summaries are contained in F. S. Regs., Part II. and the Staff Manual respectively. Title pages will be prepared in manuscript.

Place	Date	Hour	Summary of Events and Information	Remarks and references to Appendices
PROYART	10.4.17		Normal parades continued. Weather continued wet. Some rain in the evening	
PROYART.	11.4.17		Normal parades continued. Weather changeable, fine periods & snow.	
PROYART.	12.4.17		The Company went a long route march. Fine, very windy early. Snow in the evening	
PROYART.	13.4.17.		Two guns were sent to relieve two guns of No 1. M.G. Company doing anti-aircraft work near FROISSY. The day was passed in emplacement construction. The weather was fine	
PROYART.	14.4.17		Normal parades continued. Football was arranged in the afternoon. The weather was fine.	
PROYART.	15.4.17		Church parade, C. of E., was held in the morning. In the evening a voluntary Presbyterian Service was arranged. It rained all day	
PROYART.	16.4.17		Normal parades were continued in the morning. In the afternoon the Coy. prepared to move. The day was fine early, wet later.	
MERICOURT SUR-SOMME	17.4.17	9.0am	The Company moved from Camp 52 and marched to Camp 5 at MERICOURT SUR-SOMME, arriving at 9.30. The remainder of the day was spent in cleaning and repairing the camp. The day was stormy and very cold. Some hail	
MERICOURT	18.4.17		Normal parades were continued. The weather was very cold and rainy. Alterations to the camp were carried out	
MERICOURT.	19.4.17		The weather was better. Open air parades were carried out. Repairs of tent flooring, &c., instruction began. The country are very sticky & the work	
MERICOURT.	20.4.17		The weather continued fine. Open air parades were carried on & courses to in M.G. & observers in the wood was begun. Inspection instruction was begun	

WAR DIARY
or
INTELLIGENCE SUMMARY.

(Erase heading not required.)

Army Form C. 2118.

Instructions regarding War Diaries and Intelligence Summaries are contained in F. S. Regs., Part II. and the Staff Manual respectively. Title pages will be prepared in manuscript.

Place	Date	Hour	Summary of Events and Information	Remarks and references to Appendices
MERICOURT-SUR-SOMME	21/4/17		Officers instruction was continued with greatest care during the week. The men took a great interest in the work and were all very keen on map reading.	
MERICOURT	22/4/17		Services for C.E. and Presbyterians were held. In the morning the Roman Catholic Officers went for a reconnoitring ride over the ground between MORCOURT and PROYART.	
MERICOURT	23/4/17		The day was devoted in open ground work in the evening the remainder of the Officers went over the ground between MORCOURT and PROYART. On this day 32 men from the Infantry, i.e. 16 from the 1st Brigade and 16 from the 2nd Brigade were attached for duty to this unit, as the establishment does not make any allowance for casualties. The unit effected the establishment at the rate of 2 per Section were issued to the unit and were Hot food containers. They were well but do not by any means take the place of the field cookers.	
MERICOURT	24/4/17		The Company in conjunction with the 1/6th W.S.L.B.H. took part in maneuvers on the ground between PROYART and MORCOURT, acting as the defence to an attack by the Brigade. Some valuable lessons as to the war of open and protective colouring were learnt, and also as to the appearance of tanks in the open. 1 gun team captured 13 prisoners. Practice in tactics was carried out by the placing of guns by the Divisional Staff. Considerable with a criticism. The casualties were nil.	
MERICOURT	25/4/17		The day was devoted to open ground work, especially advancing over difficult open ground. The attack schemes were gone specially through.	

WAR DIARY
or
INTELLIGENCE SUMMARY.

(Erase heading not required.)

Army Form C. 2118.

Place	Date	Hour	Summary of Events and Information	Remarks and references to Appendices
MERICOURT SUR SOMME	26.4.17		The Company did a Concentration march by Sections. All rode up to time except one which had come very rough ground to cover and was 10 minutes late. The Company then took up a defensive position on ETINEHEM, under observation from the S. bank of the SOMME. This was highly successful. Contact was still maintained by the men who had just been learning Morse signalling.	JD/2 JD.2
MERICOURT	27.4.17		The day was passed in normal parades. The weather was warm & fine.	JD.2
MERICOURT	28.4.17		The day was passed in normal parades and inspections. Football was arranged for the afternoon and a match in conjunction with the 6th WELSH, in the evening. The day was very warm and fine. The subsection on duty at FROISSY was relieved by C Section.	JD.?
MERICOURT	29.4.17		Church Parades for C.of E., R.C. & Non conformists were arranged. The day was fine & warm.	JD.2
MERICOURT	30.4.17		Normal Parades, including Infantry Section practice, were carried out.	JD.2
			The remort carried by this month was employed almost entirely in training for open attack. This training was carried by notes an experience gained in recent operations. Towards the end of the month a good deal of time was spent on the training of the N.C.Os & men - the use of ground, very stern use of ground, very stern use of machine guns.	JD.2

30.4.17

J.G. Owne
O.C.
216th [Coy]

Army Form C. 2118.

No. 246 M.G.C.
Vol 3

WAR DIARY
or
INTELLIGENCE SUMMARY.

(Erase heading not required.)

Place	Date	Hour	Summary of Events and Information	Remarks and references to Appendices
MERICOURT SUR SOMME	1.5.17		The day was passed in normal parades. The G.S.O.2 came & lectured the Officers in the afternoon on the tactics of the M.G. Coy. in modern attack, which was afterwards discussed with the view to illustrating the subject. It was arranged to illustrate the scheme mentioned above by carrying out parades.	SSO
MERICOURT	2.5.17		The day was passed in normal parades. It was arranged to carry out the scheme mentioned above in conjunction with some of the officers.	SSO
MERICOURT	3.5.17		The day was passed in normal parades. The Officers went over the ground & which it is proposed to manoeuvre, & had arrangements were made with the general staff. As the weather was so warm battling was started in the Somme.	SSO
MERICOURT	4.5.17		A Tactical scheme was carried out to illustrate the employment of machine guns in the attack. The guns moved close behind the Infantry & assisted them if they were held up. Finally, when the objective was gained, taking up a position line in front. The remainder was employed in direct and indirect overhead fire, being moved up as soon as the objective was taken. The scheme was very partially successful, chiefly owing to the approachable of the lines by stages.	SSO
MERICOURT	5.5.17		The day was passed in normal parades. The weather continued to be very hot and sultry, but a terrific thunderstorm burst later & continued all night.	SSO
MERICOURT	6.5.17		Church Parade was arranged for C. & E. and non Communists. The day was fine but windy.	SSO
MERICOURT	7.5.17		The morning was passed in normal parades. At night a tactical scheme was carried out. The G.S.O.1 attended. The necessity for further training in this direction was brought to light.	SSO

Army Form C. 2118.

WAR DIARY
or
INTELLIGENCE SUMMARY.
(Erase heading not required.)

Instructions regarding War Diaries and Intelligence Summaries are contained in F.S. Regs., Part II. and the Staff Manual respectively. Title pages will be prepared in manuscript.

Places	Date	Hour	Summary of Events and Information	Remarks and references to Appendices
MERICOURT-SUR-SOMME	8.5.17		The day was passed in normal parades and lectures & the previous nights operations & daily voluntary series of lectures to N.C.Os. was started all day, but no one came in the evening. It rained hard.	
MERICOURT	9.5.17		The day was passed in normal parades and range work. The results at the table were quite good. Heard A.E. Sylvester returned from hospital.	
MERICOURT	10.5.17		The day was passed in normal parades and range work. The weather was very hot again.	
MERICOURT	11.5.17		The day was employed on a Tactical Scheme in conjunction with the 1st Bde, with Scots & Observers (inf) & M.G. Coys. The G.O.C. in C.O. was forward all guns came very helpful advice on open advances. Several points were learned on this scheme.	
MERICOURT	12.5.17		The day was passed in normal parades & battle & night compass march was carried out at night. The Sanitation Officer inspected the Camp.	
MERICOURT	13.5.17		Services of C.of E., R.C., & Presbyterians were arranged. The day was fine, with some thunderstorm in the evening.	
MERICOURT	14.5.17		The day was passed in normal parades. Preparations were made for the demonstration to be given on the 17th inst.	
MERICOURT	15.5.17		The day was passed in normal parades. In the afternoon a preliminary practice for the demonstration on the 17th was held, it was fairly successful.	
MERICOURT	16.5.17		A tactical scheme was held. The Company in conjunction with the 1st Northants had found the enemy. An attack was made by the 1st Bde. Several good targets, chiefly parties in forms, presented themselves. Had the day been finer M.G. fire would have been represented by heliography. Rain prevented this & the enemy left to imagination.	

WAR DIARY
or
INTELLIGENCE SUMMARY.
(Erase heading not required.)

Army Form C. 2118.

Instructions regarding War Diaries and Intelligence Summaries are contained in F.S. Regs., Part II. and the Staff Manual respectively. Title pages will be prepared in manuscript.

Place	Date	Hour	Summary of Events and Information	Remarks and references to Appendices
MERICOURT-SUR-SOMME	17.5.17		The morning was spent in baths, normal parades, and preparing for the demonstration. In the afternoon a demonstration in certain fire effect was given. Detail ad. was with obtained are given elsewhere. The demonstration was attended by G.O.C. 1st Division, the Bde. Genl. Commdg. 1st, 2nd, and 3rd Bdes, the Corps M.G.O. and another (as representatives of 1st Battn. commdg. in the 1st Divsn., Divsn. MBde. G. gunner, and other officers and M.G.C. Officers, N.C.Os. and men. The demonstration was successful. 1 R.A.M.C. man was attached from the Division for duty with the unit. The Company was up to full strength.	Tr. Appendix "A"
MERICOURT	18.5.17		The day was spent in normal parades, cleaning the camp and packing up. Two Sections went out to co-operate with the 10th GLOUCESTERS and 8th BERKS with the 1st Bde.	TBR
MERICOURT — VILLERS BRETONNEUX	19.5.17	2.0 p.m	The morning was passed in packing up. The Company moved off to the 9th Bde. starting point. On the way from unto the 26th Coy R.E. who, though behind the Coy in the scheduled order of march, was ahead of arrivals at the starting point 3 minutes before. Consequently the Company was late and eventually was put in the line of march in the middle of the 1st Bde. The Company arrived in billets at 5.15 p.m. The billets were fairly good. No of men falling out :— 1 with heat trouble & 2 with stomach trouble, these joining the same evening & with half these returned to the T.O.P.M. Lieut HANCOCK went on a M.G. Course at CAMIERS.	TBR
VILLERS-BRETONNEUX	20.5.17		The day was spent in Church Parades and inspections.	TBR

A5834 Wt. W4973/M687 750,000 8/16 D.D. & L. Ltd. Forms/C.2118/13.

Army Form C. 2118.

WAR DIARY
or
INTELLIGENCE SUMMARY.
(Erase heading not required.)

Instructions regarding War Diaries and Intelligence Summaries are contained in F.S. Regs., Part II. and the Staff Manual respectively. Title pages will be prepared in manuscript.

Place	Date	Hour	Summary of Events and Information	Remarks and references to Appendices
VILLERS-BRETONNEUX	20.5.17		The Company went a route march to FOUILLOY where they had dinners and bathed. The Transport was moved for the ground.	See
VILLERS-BRETONNEUX	22.5.17		The day was spent in normal parades. 2/Lieut K.L. CARRUTHERS joined the Company as 11th Officer to the Company. In the evening preliminary gates for the Divisional Sports were held amongst the Divisional troops. The (Cy) was unsuccessful.	See
VILLERS-BRETONNEUX	23.5.17		The Company went a route march to AUBERCOURT where they had dinners and bathed. A competition was held among the Sections in preparing a limber for the Divisional Sports. "A" Section won.	See
VILLERS-BRETONNEUX	24.5.17		The morning was spent in normal parades. In the afternoon the Divisional Sports was held. The Company was entered in several events but failed to bring off the prize.	See
VILLERS-BRETONNEUX	25.5.17		The day was spent in normal parades.	See
VILLERS-BRETONNEUX	26.5.17		The morning was passed in normal parades. The afternoon was spent in bathing	See
MOVING	27.5.17	8.30 a.m. 9.00 a.m. 2.14 p.m.	The Transport moved off en route for GUILLAUCOURT. The Company moved to GUILLAUCOURT, arriving at 11.15 a.m. They proceeded to entrain and trucks. The train moved off via AMIENS, ABBEVILLE, ETAPLES, BOULOGNE, CALAIS, ST OMER, HAZEBROUCK and arrived at CAESTRE	See
BERTHEN	28.5.17	3.15 a.m. 6.0 a.m.	The Company detrained and had breakfast outside the station. The Company moved to PIEBROUCK FARM 1 mile S.W. of BERTHEN. In the afternoon the C.O. was taken round anti-aircraft positions in the X Corps area to be taken up by the Company.	See

Army Form C. 2118.

WAR DIARY
or
INTELLIGENCE SUMMARY.
(Erase heading not required.)

Instructions regarding War Diaries and Intelligence Summaries are contained in F. S. Regs., Part II. and the Staff Manual respectively. Title pages will be prepared in manuscript.

Place	Date	Hour	Summary of Events and Information	Remarks and references to Appendices
BERTHEN - HEKSKEN	29.5.17		The Section were despatched to 16 anti-aircraft positions guarding camps in the vicinity of BERINGHE, VLAMERTINGHE, WESTOUTRE areas when they proceeded without mounting the guns. Coy. Hd. Qrs. moved to HEKSKEN and found practically no accommodation that eventually found a place in IX Corps area, returned then finding to them instructions. Two gun positions in the neighbourhood of VLAMERTINGHE come under shell fire	
WESTOUTRE	30.5.17		The day was passed in normal parades and attempting to find a place to settle down in. Some gun positions came under shell fire during the night.	
WESTOUTRE	31.5.17		The day was passed in normal parades. Permission was finally obtained to remain in WESTOUTRE area. Gun positions again came under shell fire during the night.	

WAR DIARY or INTELLIGENCE SUMMARY

Army Form C. 2118.

216 MG Coy Vol 4

Place	Date	Hour	Summary of Events and Information	Remarks and references to Appendices
WESTOUTRE	1.6.17		The day was passed in normal parades. The gun positions at OUDERDOM & VLAMERTINGHE again came under shell fire	JGP
WESTOUTRE	2.6.17		The day was passed in normal parades. The gun positions at OUDERDOM & VLAMERTINGHE again came under shell fire	JGP
WESTOUTRE	3.6.17		Church Parade C of E. Remainder of day passed in normal parades	JGP
WESTOUTRE	4.6.17		The day was passed in normal parades. The gun positions at OUDERDOM came under shell fire	JGP
WESTOUTRE	5.6.17		The day was passed in normal parades. The O.C. went out to the FORWARD AREA with G.S.O.1	JGP
WESTOUTRE	6.6.17		The day was passed in normal parades. The gun positions at POPERINGHE, OUDERDOM came under shell fire	JGP
WESTOUTRE	7.6.17		The day was passed in normal parades. The gun positions at POPERINGHE, OUDERDOM and VLAMERTINGHE came under shell fire	JGP
WESTOUTRE	8.6.17		The day was passed in normal parades	JGP
WESTOUTRE	9.6.17		The day was passed in normal parades	JGP
WESTOUTRE	10.6.17		The day was passed in normal parades	JGP
WESTOUTRE	11.6.17		The day was passed in normal parades	JGP
WESTOUTRE – WALLEN CAPEL	12.6.17	9 a.m. 3.30 p.m.	The guns were assembled at Coy. Hd. Qrs. All other equipment in addition to that worn was loaded on limbs. Command and the Company marched via BERTHEN, FLETRE, CAESTRE to a farm 200 yds west of HAZEBROUCK arriving 9.45 p.m.	JGP
HAZEBROUCK and WALLEN CAPEL area	13.6.17		The day was passed in cleaning up and in checking all arms and equipment. In the morning there was a demonstration at the 5th Army Workshops R.E. at HAZEBROUCK. It is about 1 block distant. The demonstration was interesting as the Workshops had only a very small Vicarette model of the M.G. to work on. A gun belonging to this unit was lent them	JGP

WAR DIARY or INTELLIGENCE SUMMARY

Army Form C. 2118.

(Erase heading not required.)

Instructions regarding War Diaries and Intelligence Summaries are contained in F.S. Regs., Part II. and the Staff Manual respectively. Title pages will be prepared in manuscript.

Place	Date	Hour	Summary of Events and Information	Remarks and references to Appendices
HAZEBROUCK WINNOLCAPELLE	14.6.17		The day was passed in enterdrains and arrival parades. The flock elsewhere was again tried at HAZEBROUCK with much better results. The gun teams were straying away again.	
WORMOUDT	15.6.17	6.30 A.M.	The Company, together with the other Brigade Companies marched via HONDEGHEM, ST SILVESTRE, TROBEGHEM, to WORMOUDT arriving 1.10 pm. The remainder of the day was spent resting.	
MALO-LES-BAINS	16.6.17	5.30 A.M.	The Company continued the march via BERGUES, HOYMILLE and BRENCHEECK. The destination was changed en route from ZUYDCOOTE to MALO-LES-BAINS. The Company was attached to 96th Brigade, 32nd Division. The Company arrived at 11.0 pm. The Billets were good but dirty.	
COXDE LES BAINS	17.6.17	11.45 A.M.	The Company proceeded by train to COXDE. From there they were sent by train to ZEPPANNES which was the original destination that to avoid the new demolitions at COXDE LES BAINS, arriving at 6.10 p.m. The O.C. (Company) went forward in advance to the front to reconnoitre positions. In the evening B Section and 4 guns relieved 4 guns withdrawn of the 114th Regt. (French) in the BEACON Sector between NIEUPORT and NIEUPORT LES BAINS. The relief passed very smoothly and without the slightest confusion. The French S.O.s conducted with every hour 2 wire gun assistance down the road.	
COXDE LES BAINS	18.6.17		The day was spent in cleaning up, reconnoitring the line. In the evening A Section relieved eight mitrailleuses of the 165th Regt (French) with 4 guns L.M.G. Sections mounted on pedestals about a mile S.E. of NIEUPORT LES BAINS. Sect STROYER (A Sector) were shot in the feet but remained at duty. Relief very satisfactory.	
NIEUPORT BAINS Trenches	19.6.17		The day passed quietly. The Depot was moved to ST IDESBALD. At night the Germans shelled the front line system, taking some prisoners. The walks were strong.	
NIEUPORT BAINS Trenches	20.6.17		This day passed quietly. Work was continued on all emplacements, and Anglos extending etc were made.	

WAR DIARY
or
INTELLIGENCE SUMMARY.

(Erase heading not required.)

Army Form C. 2118.

Place	Date	Hour	Summary of Events and Information	Remarks and references to Appendices
NIEUPORT BAINS Trenches	21.6.17		The day passed quietly. Headquarters were moved up to the right of the nearest line, together with the 8 guns of C & D Sections. These were kept in reserve and not in action. The D.O.C. Engineer was appointed Divisional M.G. Officer of Division.	J09
NIEUPORT BAINS Trenches	22.6.17		The day passed quietly. Work was in progress on all shelters construction than for our men. The shelter was moved to LE FEVRE CAMPS between Oost DUNKERQUE BAINS and COXYDE BAINS. 2nd Lieut. BROWNE went & 2nd Lieut of C Sect to hospital. 1st Division. Wsth.	J09
NIEUPORT BAINS	23.6.17		The day was quiet. The Sergeant Commander was posted M.G. from lines. 16.th evening 3 guns of D Section came into position on the corner, and one gun of A Section were withdrawn. One gun of C Section relieved one gun of B which was with dissatisfied and the guns of C Section came into position. Remaining guns of B, S were withdrawn.	J09
NIEUPORT BAINS Trenches	24.6.17		Rest was slight hostile artillery activity Cy. and Gns. was moved into NIEUPORT BAINS. Work was continued Thursday wealth.	J09
NIEUPORT BAINS Trenches	25.6.17		Considerable hostile artillery activity on the strain back NIEUPORT-BAINS. The nearest gun of C Section in action was moved up to the line with the remainder, there being the main work was continued.	J00
NIEUPORT BAINS Trenches	26.6.17		The day was very quiet. Nothing of particular importance occurred. Work was continued.	J09
NIEUPORT BAINS Trenches	27.6.17		Heavy hostile bombardment of our line E. of the river. No of the bridges kind. No damage done to the guns. Later in evening a fourth gun of D Section was put in. the line.	J09
NIEUPORT BAINS Trenches	28.6.17		A very quiet day of disturbance occurred. There was an intermittent enemy relief at night strong rain throughout.	J09
NIEUPORT BAINS	29.6.17		A quiet day. Two aeroplanes appeared over our lines and were shot at with rifles.	J.C.
NIEUPORT BAINS	30.6.17		A very quiet day. Walla and very showy apparently now taken of course. Not to examine all loopholes by day light. Many of them had no castled floors, and after the snow was loosened the sand fell below, which would have jammed the gun. Any breakages necessary alterations were carried out at night.	J.C.

WAR DIARY
or
INTELLIGENCE SUMMARY

Army Form C. 2118.

Place	Date	Hour	Summary of Events and Information	Remarks and references to Appendices
NIEUPORT BAINS	30 June 1917		Summary of events for JUNE. The first part of the month passed exceedingly quietly. The guns were distributed amongst various dumps to minimise possible loss. Little in the way of training was possible. The Coy was busy in the battle for the MESSINES – WYTSCHAETE Ridge, which only affected the Company by preventing further shelling of the dumps. A stile of more followed during which time was not found to get the Company together, cleaned & checked & made fit for events. The relief of the Division on the sea-coast then brought a good deal of interest. It was softly remarkable for the completeness of the arrangement & also so far as M.Gs were concerned, at the absence of all action during actual relief — this in spite of the fact that 1 of our Officers was wounded during it, and his N.C.O. had to carry on. When the British were settled in on the coast the enemy gradually increased his activity till it reached a culminating point in the bombardment of Bns. 27th & that down again in the immediate quiet of the last three days of the month. Lt Conway Major 216th M.G.Coy	

Army Form C. 2118.

WAR DIARY
or
INTELLIGENCE SUMMARY.
(Erase heading not required.)

Instructions regarding War Diaries and Intelligence Summaries are contained in F. S. Regs., Part II. and the Staff Manual respectively. Title pages will be prepared in manuscript.

Place	Date	Hour	Summary of Events and Information	Remarks and references to Appendices
TRENCHES NIEUPORT BAINS	1.7.17		Mobile artillery active, but especially near the bridgehead. Work on all emplacements continued.	JRO
NIEUPORT BAINS	2.7.17		Situation as yesterday. Work continued. Several indirect fire positions sited. 1st Blockhouse carried out a successful raid at night.	JRO
NIEUPORT BAINS	3.7.17		Situation as usual. Work continued on indirect fire positions etc. Raid at Nieuport by 8th Rifles, but not brought off. The support battalion was relieved.	JRO
NIEUPORT BAINS	4.7.17		Situation as usual. Work continued as on 3rd. Battalions in the front line were relieved. A series of raids carried out on 3rd.	JRO
NIEUPORT BAINS	5.7.17		Slight increase in hostile artillery activity. Work continued on indirect fire positions. An alternative position constructed in the west.	JRO
NIEUPORT BAINS	6.7.17		Hostile artillery very active on W bank of the YSER, especially round the Station. Work continued. One M.G. casualty.	JRO
NIEUPORT BAINS	7.7.17		No decrease in hostile artillery activity. This continued increasingly all day. The night comparatively quiet.	JRO
NIEUPORT BAINS	8.7.17		The weather changed, the day was dull though our back areas were very fine on W bank of YSER. There was not far the enemy, but for the aeroplanes the guns from would almost very little chance. There was an extraordinary quiet all not M.G. shot to be heard.	JRO
NIEUPORT BAINS	9.7.17		Increase in hostile activity in the morning. Communication trenches to front line Station and MAISON DE MARINS blown in. A partially successful raid was made by the 8th KRR's, coming through.	JRO
NIEUPORT BAINS	10.7.17		A very heavy bombardment began at 10 a.m. and was carried on through the day towards midday all an intense barrage was placed roughly about the NIEUPORT BAINS — NIEUPORT railway. About 1.0 p.m. this barrage lifted and rested on the sea. At about 2.0 gradually assembly troops of the enemy. At about 3.30 p.m. the SOS became very intense. A barrage was placed on the line NIEUPORT BAINS — NIEUPORT BAINS STATION — the railway.	JRO

A 5834 Wt W4973 M68· 750,000 8/16 D. D. & L. Ltd. Forms/C.2118/13.

Army Form 2118.

WAR DIARY
or
INTELLIGENCE SUMMARY.
(Erase heading not required.)

[Stamp: MACHINE GUN CORPS No. 216 COY]

Place	Date	Hour	Summary of Events and Information	Remarks and references to Appendices
NIEUPORT BAINS	10.7.17		At 7.30 a.m. a message was received from the 1st L.N. Lancs that the front line was the W. bank of the YSER. Arrangements at once made to visit the guns and see that everything was in order. The Station patrols were found to be in good order inside the guncotton. Lieut R.G. Wilson fortunately succeeded in getting three guns into action in spite of the heavy bombardment going on in the neighbourhood. BULLPITT had moved his way to the gun W. of the sea head after time 3/guns an officer of the 2nd R. Sussex in charge of the 37 mm guns. He signalled a runner across post at the W. end of the bridge nearer the sea. Communication with the guns in the right subsects was cut off by a heavy barrage along the only line of communication. All runners were called up, with instructions to relieve the right, 3 in number on the left; there was also several temporarily used one officer from No. 2 M.G. Coy who had lost all their guns. These runners with not wanted eventually. By midnight matters were settling down but the state of the new front line was not known very clearly.	[initial]
	11.7.17		About 1.30 a.m. the enemy sent up a string of orange lights and artillery fire then slackened. About considerably. 3 Officers of the 2nd K.R.R.'s, 1st No.2 M.G. Coy. This had no casualties approximately 40 O.R. from various units 1st Australian Tunnelling Office 6.d. approximately the river reached the bank. They were able to split a certain amount of information. The Germans were evidently a bit back of the river bank, but were considerably a bit back for it. About 6.0 a.m. a message was received from the gun crew stating there has been a very intense bombardment throughout all the	[initial]

WAR DIARY
or
INTELLIGENCE SUMMARY.
(Erase heading not required.)

Army Form C. 2118.

Place	Date	Hour	Summary of Events and Information	Remarks and references to Appendices
NIEUPORT BAINS	11.7.17		M.G. emplacements were still standing. There was only one casualty through the day, due to shell fire. Gun had been replaced by the reserve gun. The raid had been carried out successfully. During the day and the time was occupied in consolidating work. 2/Lt A.C. CRAWFORD wounded but remained on duty, 1 O.R. killed, 1 missing, 4 wounded. The night of the day proved very quiet. Between the hrs of 10/11 and 11th/12th there were considerable trouble from the Germans with rifle and M.G. fire. Two of the guns firing across the river had been in action. Rifle and M.G. emplacements had caused of annoyance, flares, very lights, all forms of parties & flares.	See
NIEUPORT BAINS	12.7.17		The day was comparatively quiet & dug-out – munipt built. Throughout the day a patrol of the K.R.R's who had been across they reported the Germans were about	See
NIEUPORT BAINS	13.7.17		The day was comparatively quiet – work continued	Oct
NIEUPORT BAINS	14.7.17		The day was comparatively quiet – work continued	Oct
NIEUPORT BAINS	15.7.17		Situation as yesterday. Work continued	Oct
NIEUPORT BAINS	16.7.17		Situation fairly quiet. Battle gas shells arriving some time.	Oct
NIEUPORT BAINS	17.7.17		The day was comparatively quiet – arrangements made ready for the Company at night. Transport leaving moved back to COXYDE	Oct
NIEUPORT BAINS COXYDE	18.7.17		Relay Company conflict – all Gun teams relieved by 5.30 am. arrangements complete for moving. Company by Route Cony. St. Px. dis-Bois Carmont and arrive	Oct

Army Form C. 2118.

WAR DIARY
or
INTELLIGENCE SUMMARY.
(Erase heading not required.)

Instructions regarding War Diaries and Intelligence Summaries are contained in F.S. Regs., Part II. and the Staff Manual respectively. Title pages will be prepared in manuscript.

[Stamp: MACHINE GUN CORPS No. 215 Coy]

Place	Date	Hour	Summary of Events and Information	Remarks and references to Appendices
ST POL	19-7-17	9:30am	Company started by march to LE CLIPON CAMP and arrived normal etc	
LE CLIPON CAMP	20.7.17		Day passed in normal parades. Weather hot. Men rather worn out after recent activities	
LE CLIPON CAMP	21.7.17		Day passed in normal parades and refitting. Company with clothing	
LE CLIPON CAMP	22.7.17		Day passed on normal parades — special attn in pains to physical fitness	
LE CLIPON CAMP	23.7.17		Day passed in normal parades and overhauling all arms, ammunition etc.	
LE CLIPON CAMP	24.7.17		Day passed in normal parades. Weather continues fine getting in good condition	
LE CLIPON CAMP	25.7.17		Day passed in normal parades. An obstacle course allotted — all ranks very keen — got round well	
LE CLIPON CAMP	26.7.17		Day passed in normal parades. Weather favourable	
LE CLIPON CAMP	27.7.17		Day passed in normal parades. Field tactics used to open fighting	
LE CLIPON CAMP	28.7.17		Day passed in normal parades. Section schemes in training area	
LE CLIPON CAMP	29.7.17		Day passed in normal parades	
LE CLIPON CAMP	30.7.17		Day passed in normal parades. Raining — went down in tents	
LE CLIPON CAMP	31.7.17		Day passed in normal parades. Some Rain	

F. Dunlop
26th July 17

Army Form C. 2118.

WAR DIARY
or
INTELLIGENCE SUMMARY.
(Erase heading not required.)

9516

Place	Date	Hour	Summary of Events and Information	Remarks and references to Appendices
LE CLIPON CAMP	1.8.17		The day was passed in normal parades. Weather dull. Range work during the forenoon	Col
LE CLIPON CAMP	2.8.17		Heavy rain, usual civilian work employed	Col
LE CLIPON CAMP	3.8.17		Heavy rain, all parades under cover. Lecture by officer	Col
LE CLIPON CAMP	4.8.17		Weather improving, some showers, outdoor training recommenced	Col
LE CLIPON CAMP	5.8.17		Church parades morning. Special Patrol Course in fighting order. Weather dull	Col
LE CLIPON CAMP	6.8.17		The day was passed in normal parades. Sunny day. Firing on range	Col
LE CLIPON CAMP	7.8.17		Weather continues good - men practised in carrying guns ammunition etc over dunes	Col
LE CLIPON CAMP	8.8.17		Day passed in parades as yesterday - experiments made with special parrier	Col
LE CLIPON CAMP	9.8.17		Weather cloudy. Company scheme to repell a landing party successfully carried out	Col
LE CLIPON CAMP	10.8.17		The day was passed in normal parades. YUKON PACKS tried with various loads	Col
LE CLIPON CAMP	11.8.17		Day passed as yesterday - Some success. Robinson Portable Rifle box	Col
LE CLIPON CAMP	12.8.17		Weather fine. Church Parades in morning	Col
LE CLIPON CAMP	13.8.17		The day was passed in normal parades - pontoon stand tower still used with good results	Col
LE CLIPON CAMP	14.8.17		Weather fine - day passed as yesterday	Col
LE CLIPON CAMP	15.8.17		Weather dull. The day was passed in normal parades	Col
LE CLIPON CAMP	16.8.17		Sun showers hit enemy aerial still planes, hand gun. Men sprinkled to green's low lying	Col

WAR DIARY or INTELLIGENCE SUMMARY

Army Form C. 2118.

(Erase heading not required.)

Instructions regarding War Diaries and Intelligence Summaries are contained in F. S. Regs., Part II. and the Staff Manual respectively. Title pages will be prepared in manuscript.

Place	Date	Hour	Summary of Events and Information	Remarks and references to Appendices
LE CLIPON CAMP	17.8.17		Weather fine. Day passed firing on range	
LE CLIPON CAMP	18.8.17		The day was passed in normal parades. Experiments made with French Bag to football & man in morning. Slung on rifle.	
LE CLIPON CAMP	19.8.17		Weather still sunny. Church Parades in morning. Afternoon football anglo-Irish.	
LE CLIPON CAMP	20.8.17		The day was passed in normal firing. French Bag Bottles and Single grass & man on Journey a Gnoves.	
LE CLIPON CAMP	21.8.17		Weather fine. Day was passed in normal parades and special vehicle course.	
LE CLIPON CAMP	22.8.17		The day was passed in special schemes in conjunction with brigade. Many points of interest brought out.	
LE CLIPON CAMP	23.8.17		Weather still fine. The day was spent firing on range. Attached men shew great improvement.	
LE CLIPON CAMP	24.8.17		Some thunder and heavy showers. The day passes in normal parades.	
LE CLIPON CAMP	25.8.17		Inspection by Army Commander Lt Genl. Presentation of medals read past 9th Division	
LE CLIPON CAMP	26.8.17		Church Parades in the morning. Afternoon football competition.	
LE CLIPON CAMP	27.8.17		Heavy thunderous weather in camp	
	28.8.17		Very wet. worked in Tents	
	29.8.17		Showers during day. normal parades	
	30.8.17		Route March	
	31.8.17		Normal Parades	

Army Form C. 2118.

216 M.G. Coy

WAR DIARY
or
INTELLIGENCE SUMMARY.
(Erase heading not required.)

Instructions regarding War Diaries and Intelligence Summaries are contained in F.S. Regs., Part II. and the Staff Manual respectively. Title pages will be prepared in manuscript.

Place	Date	Hour	Summary of Events and Information	Remarks and references to Appendices
Le Clipon Camp	1.9.17		Weather fine. The day was spent in normal parades	
Le Clipon Camp	2.9.17		Morning church parade. Recreation in the afternoon.	
Le Clipon Camp	3.9.17		Weather continues fine. Several changes in our lost of Officers posted and in-coming listed.	
Le Clipon Camp	4.9.17		The day was passed in normal parades. Weather continued.	
Le Clipon Camp	5.9.17		Weather dull. The day was passed in usual manner.	
Le Clipon Camp	6.9.17		The weather took a turn of the worse. Rained in a few days. Several men posted to Company in Base.	
Le Clipon Camp	7.9.17		Weather fine. The day passed in normal parades and special stokes course.	
Le Clipon Camp	8.9.17		Morning passed in special lectures and Pelham. Afternoon Company in the 3 platoons.	
Le Clipon Camp	9.9.17		Morning church parade. Afternoon recreation.	
Le Clipon Camp	10.9.17		Weather fine. The day was passed in normal parades.	
Le Clipon Camp	11.9.17		Weather fine. The day was passed in the usual manner.	
Le Clipon Camp	12.9.17		Morning passed in normal parades and special stokes course. Afternoon spent in 3 platoons attacked. Entertaining.	
Le Clipon Camp	13.9.17		Weather continues very wet. Firing in range and visits ready to tender	
Le Clipon Camp	14.9.17		The day was passed in normal musketry parade.	
Le Clipon Camp	15.9.17		Morning spent in ordinary parades. Afternoon recreation.	
Le Clipon Camp	16.9.17		Weather fine. Morning church parade.	
Le Clipon Camp	17.9.17		The day was spent in normal parades and special stokes course.	

Army Form C. 2118.

WAR DIARY
or
INTELLIGENCE SUMMARY.
(Erase heading not required.)

Instructions regarding War Diaries and Intelligence Summaries are contained in F. S. Regs., Part II. and the Staff Manual respectively. Title pages will be prepared in manuscript.

Place	Date	Hour	Summary of Events and Information	Remarks and references to Appendices
LE CLIPON CAMP	18.9.17		Special scheme with infantry. B & C sections with 2nd Bn Royal Sussex and A & D sections with 1 E.L.N. Lancs.	PRW
LE CLIPON CAMP	19.9.17		A & D sections offensive action with 1st Gloucestershire Regt in defence against 1st Brigade (2 landing PWs) B & C sections route march.	PRW
LE CLIPON CAMP	20.9.17		Weather continues fine. Normal parades in morning. Recreation in afternoon.	PRW
LE CLIPON CAMP	21.9.17		Ordinary parades & obstacle course in morning. Heats for sports run off in afternoon.	PRW
LE CLIPON CAMP	22.9.17		M.G.C. 1st Div Sports on 1st Bde Sports Ground.	PRW
LE CLIPON CAMP	23.9.17		Church parade in the morning. Weather rather dull.	PRW
LE CLIPON CAMP	24.9.17		Normal parades in the morning; bathing parade in afternoon.	PRW
LE CLIPON CAMP	25.9.17		Weather very warm. The day was spent in ordinary parades.	PRW
LE CLIPON CAMP	26.9.17		Normal parades including practice in barrage drill & special obstacle course.	PRW
LE CLIPON CAMP	27.9.17		Tactical Exercise with 6th Welsh Regt & 1coy 10th Gloster.	PRW
LE CLIPON CAMP	28.9.17		Weather continues fine, the day passed in normal parades.	PRW
LE CLIPON CAMP	29.9.17		The day was passed in normal parades & special obstacle course.	PRW
LE CLIPON CAMP	30.9.17		Weather hot. Morning Church parade, afternoon recreation.	PRW

WAR DIARY
or
INTELLIGENCE SUMMARY.

(Erase heading not required.)

Army Form C. 2118.

216 M.G. Coy

Instructions regarding War Diaries and Intelligence Summaries are contained in F. S. Regs., Part II. and the Staff Manual respectively. Title pages will be prepared in manuscript.

Place	Date	Hour	Summary of Events and Information	Remarks and references to Appendices
LE CLIPON CAMP	1.10.17		Weather hot. The day was passed in route march & taking parade	
LE CLIPON CAMP	2.10.17		The day was passed in normal parades — physical attention being paid to Barrage Fire Drill	
LE CLIPON CAMP	3.10.17		Weather continues fine — The day passed was and 2nd Brigade in special operations	
LE CLIPON CAMP	4.10.17		The morning spent in normal parades, training parties for night operations	
LE CLIPON CAMP	5.10.17		Weather dull. day was passed in operations with 3rd Brigade	
LE CLIPON CAMP	6.10.17		Weather stormy. The day was passed in normal parades	
LE CLIPON CAMP	7.10.17		Weather wet & boisterous. Church Parades — afternoon recreation	
LE CLIPON CAMP	8.10.17		Weather fine. The morning was passed in normal parades — training parties for night operations	
LE CLIPON CAMP	9.10.17		The day was passed in normal parades	
LE CLIPON CAMP	10.10.17		Weather wet. Some Sections The day passed on normal parades	
LE CLIPON CAMP	11.10.17		Raining. The day passed as normal parades, night operations situation	
LE CLIPON CAMP	12.10.17		Raining The day was spent in normal parades. afternoon listen to views by 2.0.C. 4th Army	
LE CLIPON CAMP	13.10.17		Raining The day passed in normal parades. O.C. had leave at 1.0. to attend conference with General Ronwashen	
LE CLIPON CAMP	14.10.17		Weather fine. Parading passed in Church Parades. afternoon recreation	
LE CLIPON CAMP	15.10.17		Weather sunny. The day was passed in normal parades	
LE CLIPON CAMP	16.10.17		Very cold. The day was passed in normal parades — special attention paid to Barrage fire and drill	
LE CLIPON CAMP	17.10.17		Fine but cold. The day was passed in normal parades. Training parties for night operations	

WAR DIARY
or
INTELLIGENCE SUMMARY.
(Erase heading not required.)

Army Form C. 2118.

Instructions regarding War Diaries and Intelligence Summaries are contained in F.S. Regs., Part II. and the Staff Manual respectively. Title pages will be prepared in manuscript.

Place	Date	Hour	Summary of Events and Information	Remarks and references to Appendices
LE CLIPON CAMP	18.10.17		Weather continues fine but cold. Morning spent in normal parades. Afternoon parades almost nil by the Company. Barrage fire G.S.O.1 was present.	
LE CLIPON CAMP	19.10.17		Weather fine — the day was spent in general lectures in the afternoon to all ranks by XV C.M.G.O. Barrage demonstration.	
LE CLIPON CAMP	20.10.17		Weather fine cold — the morning spent in normal parades. Afternoon Barrage fire scheme.	
LE CLIPON CAMP	21.10.17		Weather as yesterday — morning church parade. Afternoon preparations for march to new area.	
LE CLIPON CAMP	22.10.17	7.45 am 3.5 pm	Company parade and transport for march to ROUBROUCK AREA. Weather fine. Company arrived in billets near ERKELSBRUGGE — men marched well.	
ERKELSBRUGGE	23.10.17		Weather wet — the day was passed in normal parades	
ERKELSBRUGGE	24.10.17		Weather fine — morning spent in normal parades — Baths — afternoon preparation for march.	
ERKELSBRUGGE	25.10.17	6.30 am 11.15 am	Company parade & march to HOUTKERQUE AREA. Weather fine from Company arrived in billets 1½ miles WEST of HOUTKERQUE, men marched well, no stragglers in the area very poor.	
HOUTKERQUE AREA	26.10.17		Weather very wet — the day was passed in normal parades. Special Section being fitted to Barrage event	
HOUTKERQUE AREA	27.10.17		Weather dull — the day was passed in normal parades.	
HOUTKERQUE AREA	28.10.17		Weather as yesterday, morning Church parade — afternoon fatigues	
HOUTKERQUE AREA	29.10.17		Weather sunny — the day was passed in scheme for BARRAGE.	
HOUTKERQUE AREA	30.10.17		Very wet — the day passed in normal parades, lectures.	
HOUTKERQUE AREA	31.10.17		Weather fine — the day was passed in normal parades.	

Army Form C. 2118.

WAR DIARY 216 M.G. Coy
or
INTELLIGENCE SUMMARY.
(Erase heading not required.)

Instructions regarding War Diaries and Intelligence Summaries are contained in F.S. Regs., Part II. and the Staff Manual respectively. Title pages will be prepared in manuscript.

Place	Date	Hour	Summary of Events and Information	Remarks and references to Appendices
HOUTKERQUE AREA	1.11.17		Weather fine – The day was passed in normal parades. C.O. and Section officers paid visits to recommended billets in Flanders.	Col
HOUTKERQUE AREA	2.11.17		Weather as yesterday – day passed in normal parades.	Col
HOUTKERQUE AREA	3.11.17		Weather very dull – day passed in normal parades. Special attention to parades & French. Foot – inspection in foot-drilling.	Col
HOUTKERQUE AREA	4.11.17		Weather fine – Morning passed in Church Parades – afternoon recreation.	Col
HOUTKERQUE AREA	5.11.17		Weather fine – day passed in normal parades and Barrage scheme.	Col
HOUTKERQUE AREA	6.11.17 11.05 a.m. 2.00 p.m.		Company Parade for move to the Poperinghe Area under 3rd Brigade arrangements. Arrived DIRTY BUCKET CAMP near POPERINGHE.	Col
DIRTY BUCKET CAMP	7.11.17 4.10 a.m. 11.10 "		C.O. took Officers to reconnoitre line. Was arranged for 3 sections of what IRISH FARM were supplying to fighting Capt HANCOCK was detailed to arrange a Barrage for the 10th using 8 guns. No 2 Coy 8 Guns No 3 Coy. 63rd Div. Position of Guns were :– B.C.D. ready for 2/8.11.17 reg. normal 8 guns 10/88 Coy. 1/2 Guns .	Col
			D. Section 2/Lieut STREET 4 Guns D.3C.2.9. firing on S.O.S. lines to V.19.b. REG MAP C. Section 2/Lt. CARPENTER 2 " BUFF HOUSE V.27.b. SH. 1ST 10,000 3. Section 2/Lt. CARR 2 " TARGET FARM V.27.c. " " " " DEWAS HOUSE V.27.a. SHORT V.27.a SOURCE TRENCH V.28.d. 2/Lieut Scott was in charge of the group of MG at HQ a/c HUNTER FARM. Relief was carried out 12.30 midnight. Kelso was carried out on 188 Coy.	
LOCARILLE				

WAR DIARY
or
INTELLIGENCE SUMMARY.

Army Form C. 2118.

(Erase heading not required.)

Place	Date	Hour	Summary of Events and Information	Remarks and references to Appendices
DIRTY BUCKET CAMP	8.11.17		Capt HANCOCK visited positions of a group of 4/2B Guns for Barrage fire to assist 3rd Canadian Infantry Brigade in their attack on the 10th inst. Two Batteries A.P.M. No 2 & B Bttn. 216 Coy reported - were billed at ZEPHYR at LEPERTRY MOLLENMOLEN D4c. One Battery No 3 Coy at YETTA HOUSE D3d. Batteries were brought into action at night. Barrage practice carried & attached was. No 1 Coy 216 Bn & Sec 2C Coy 216 Streets were taken over Batty "B" Bttn. H.Q. & Capt HANCOCK's billet at [??] Farm D33c9. "B" Group of 4 Defensive Group D16b & initial schedule barrage arranged (Barrage Fire Commander — Lt Carruthers) the guns being to front and rear.	(Sgd)
DIRTY BUCKET CAMP	9.11.17		Barrage Fire	1 - Battery Commanders Issued :- "A" Batty. 2/Lt WEBB No 2 N.C.O. Coy No 1 2/Lt SIMS No 2 2/Lt MEADOWS "B" Batty. 2/Lt BROWNE HOLD No 1 2/Lt CRAFFORD No 2 2/Lt STREETS "C" Batty No 1 2/Lt PROGERSON No 3 2/Lt MARKS No 2 2/Lt SUMNER Telephonic communication was established between Batteries Coy HANCOCK'S Group O.C. Barrage Group KRUMBINZ FARM & from there to Major HONAIRE O.C. M.G. Group on the line of 3rd Infantry Brigade R.S.P. R.O.I.203 area. Forders were issued. Letters issued to all Ruling and known guns laid on the defensive Barrage lines Barrage lines :- "A" Batty 1/3 19.13 Batteries "A" Batty V23 a 20.05 & V30a 05.87 - root bay Bound B. "B" Batty V23 c 45.23 & V23 a 24.05 - Supply roof to Baun & S.O.S. line at V23 a 43.05 to V23 c 27.05 "C" Batty V23 a 55.12 & V23 c 27.05 - S.O.S line at V22 d 80.75 & V23 a 05.05 Defensive Group - Schedule barrage — 4 guns working Maxim Wiring B. Lt. K.L. Carruthers. Details arranged in the Force to take the	(Sgd)

Army Form C. 2118.

WAR DIARY
or
INTELLIGENCE SUMMARY.
(Erase heading not required.)

Instructions regarding War Diaries and Intelligence Summaries are contained in F. S. Regs., Part II. and the Staff Manual respectively. Title pages will be prepared in manuscript.

Place	Date	Hour	Summary of Events and Information	Remarks and references to Appendices
DIRTY BUCKET CAMP	10.11.17		The 3rd Canadian Infy Brigade were attacking Passchendaele Ridge from TOURNANT & EAST of VOCATION FARM. V.29.d.2. V.10.b.15,75 respectively. They moved into the TRENCHES	
		2500 HOUR 6.15 Am	The Z+3 Kc M.G Barrage commenced and continued until Z+4/30 firing 60 rounds per gun per minute and from Z+43 to Z+1/20 at 30-45 per minute. [illegible handwriting continues]	Ok
DIRTY BUCKET CAMP	11.11.17		The Barrage Battery withdrew to DIRTY BUCKET CAMP. Barrage's work was accomplished with no definite casualties. [illegible]	Ok
DIRTY BUCKET CAMP	12.11.17	8.35 pm	Bay Coy moved Hooge + L.Track - 9 guns + Wye Coy moved to Haul 2 guns to the huts on the recovery of L13.X	Ok
DIRTY BUCKET CAMP	13.11.17	7.30 pm	Lt BULLPITT + 2 Fry Ians + 50 O.R. moved into billets at KANSAS HOUSE & Mr ANGELL O.C M.G's in the Zone. They lay overnight & Mr YETTA HOUSE pending [illegible]	Ok
DIRTY BUCKET CAMP	14.11.17	7.15 pm	[illegible] other ranks by Lampton & Hamburg arrived YETTA HOUSE on 14. Western Coy Lampton Hull Richmond + Bow [illegible] 1st Fry + 74 + 2 Fry Ians at YETTA HOUSE pending [illegible] to Ka[illegible] and at WILSON on Relief. Capt CRAWFORD took 24 [illegible] of Reserve Company	Ok

Army Form C. 2118.

WAR DIARY
or
INTELLIGENCE SUMMARY.
(Erase heading not required.)

Instructions regarding War Diaries and Intelligence Summaries are contained in F.S. Regs., Part II. and the Staff Manual respectively. Title pages will be prepared in manuscript.

Place	Date	Hour	Summary of Events and Information	Remarks and references to Appendices
DIRTY BUCKET CAMP	15.11.17		2/Lt BULPITT + his team relieved 2/Lt No 1 Fog 2/Lt KENT + his team. S.O.S signal at 5.30 am during shift at Jan 24. Shelling at 1700. Casualties 2 O.R. killed. Camp shelled during night range H.V. guns	
DIRTY BUCKET CAMP	16.11.17		Keeping D.M.G.O. called + gave notice for 4 guns to proceed immediately to YETTA HOUSE — those under 2/Lt BROWNE proceeded at 2.30 pm — 21 Reinforcements arrived from base — took line	
DIRTY BUCKET CAMP	17.11.17		2/Lt STROVER and 4 teams proceeded to YETTA HOUSE and joined 2/Lt BROWNE forming a battery 8 guns firing on S.O.S. lines when visual signal offered. Situation normal	
DIRTY BUCKET CAMP	18.11.17		2/Lt CARLISLE + 1/Lt CARR relieved the battery in the line — situation quiet. Arrangements made for Carrying hot tea for teams in the line. The special carriers attached to the Company need to be their gunfire. The battery were not called upon to fire near HONSTAS CORNER + O.R. killed. 2 during relief while relieving — Whilst landing on the trip near HONSTAS HOUSE 2	
DIRTY BUCKET CAMP	19.11.17		The battery not called on to fire on S.O.S. lines — situation quiet. Tea arrangements working satisfactorily — men greatly comforted	
DIRTY BUCKET CAMP	20.11.17		2/Lt WILSON + 2/Lt BULPITT relieved battery in the line — situation quiet no shelling on position Cpl J.R HOWARD wounded M.M. No S.O.S. call	
DIRTY BUCKET CAMP	21.11.17		Situation normal — no S.O.S. call. YETTA HOUSE Battery position still unharmed by enemy	
DIRTY BUCKET CAMP	22.11.17		2/Lt BROWNE & 2/Lt STROVER relieved battery on the line — situation quiet — relief completed satisfactorily. No S.O.S. call. Teams enjoying hostels pleasure	
DIRTY BUCKET CAMP	23.11.17		Situation quiet — work continued as before. Very useful things recovered + dug out. Salvage parties organized Company relieved by 219 Company — left camp at Elverde Ranelde over	
DIRTY BUCKET CAMP	24.11.17		Company horses 12.30 pm for move to TUNNELLING CAMP which was reached 2.30 pm SHEET 27 NW4 F 27 a	

WAR DIARY
or
INTELLIGENCE SUMMARY.

(Erase heading not required.)

Army Form C. 2118.

Place	Date	Hour	Summary of Events and Information	Remarks and references to Appendices
TUNNELLING CAMP Ref Sheet 27. 40,000	25-11-17		The day was spent cleaning, checking guns, equipment etc. Weather fine.	Ref
TUNNELLING CAMP	26-11-17		Weather cold. Company inspected for deficiencies in clothing, kit etc. General clean up ordered. Orders received for move to CANADA CAMP	Ref
TUNNELLING CAMP	27-11-17	2.15pm	Company hands over move to CANADA CAMP Sheet 27 40,000 F16a which was reached 4.30pm PROHERZ AREA. Weather fine, accommodation good.	Ref
Sheet 27 40,000 F16a	28-11-17		Weather very dull - the day was passed in normal parades	Ref
PROHERZ AREA	29-11-17		Weather fine - the day was passed in normal parades. 21 O.R. reinforcements arrived	Ref
PROHERZ AREA	30-11-17		Weather as yesterday - the day passed in normal parades. Lt/Col HANCOCK and Lt CLARKE left 2.0.2 pm to reconnoitre the line	Ref

Army Form C. 2118.

WAR DIARY
or
INTELLIGENCE SUMMARY.
(Erase heading not required.)

Instructions regarding War Diaries and Intelligence Summaries are contained in F.S. Regs., Part II. and the Staff Manual respectively. Title pages will be prepared in manuscript.

Place	Date	Hour	Summary of Events and Information	Remarks and references to Appendices
PROHERZ AREA Sheet 27 1/40,000 E.16.c.l.	1.12.17		Capt. HANCOCK granted special leave U.K. with Section. Lt. CATCHPOLE assumes command. Two Recruits arrived in form of Reinforcements from Corps in 2 days. N.C.O. & 4 Men sent to R.F.C.	Ref
PROHERZ AREA	2.12.17		Weather fine. Morning Church Parade. Afternoon Lecture - Limbers & dismounting. Orders received for 2 Sections to proceed to front line.	Ref
PROHERZ AREA	3.12.17	4.45am	Lt. CATCHPOLE, Lt. CARLILE, 1st M.G.CORR. with "A" & "B" Sections left for WOESTEN AREA in 3rd army. West in charge & Lt. WOESTEN AREA. Old attached Cameron accompany this party. Limbers returned party.	Ref
WOESTEN AREA	4.12.17	2.0pm	Lt. CARLILE & Lt. CHARR 8 Gun team moved to WOESTEN AREA to relieve 8 Guns of the 2nd French Division by Alphonse Ferdin on SOUTH side of the BROENBEEK RIVER. Relief very successful. Great Care taken by French Posters of Guns.	
			— 2 Guns at V.15.b.12 (MAP REFS)
			— 2 " at V.15.a.67 } 28 N.W. 1
			— 2 " at V.8.d.27 } 20 S.W. 20.000 O.C. No.1 M.G.Coy
			SECTION H.Q. DUNDONALDBERT FARM — 2 at V.7.d.71
WOESTEN AREA	5.12.17	7.30pm	Lt. Chakoy & No.2 Section moved to WOESTEN AREA where they arrived 11.30am. Long Coy accommodation found at MARIE FARM. Telephonic Communication installed R.1st DIVISION T.M.B. at Transport H.Q. at EYKHOEK. S.21.a with 1st Brigade Machine Guns
MARIE FARM	6.12.17		Lt. CATCHPOLE & Lt. BROWNE left to reconnoitre the 8 Guns in the line. Two Coys to be held for ready occupation. Raining on Brass Guns in corner of Rent hedge & Brass Posts ready.	Ref
SHEET 20 - 40.000			PILLBOXES defensive belt of wire laid out. Also S.O.S. lines arranged. Ration party & also LANCER CROSS ROADS to mile cycle. Communication available by means of DUNIP FARM T.27
			Two R.A. Guns were seen in rear of Btn. H.Q. WOESTEN.
MARIE FARM	7.12.17		Relief reported to have to 2 Guns at V.15.12 to an old German Encampment at V.8.a.45.5 East to S.W. Coys in billets, weather cold & very wet.	Ref
			Visit to old aid post & the Asiatic was made by Young very good Observation to BROENBEEK & the Area beyond. BIXSCHOOTE
			Communication from MARIE FARM to line by cycles.
MARIE FARM	8.12.17		Hard day work. Lt. Gunn with 2 Guns N. of the BROENBEEK 2 Guns from U.9 C.57.12. Pill Boxes sites were very rich. 2 " " U.8.d.80.40	Ref
			Raining & cold. Orders received to stand to for any attack.	
MARIE FARM	9.12.17		Fine & sunny. Guns moved forward undisturbed. Sites same.	Ref
MARIE FARM	10.12.17		Front Arty Coys pass R.L. BIXSCHOOTE & pushed forward a few yards reinforced by M.G.fire at V.8.a.45. Enemy retired.
			Weather stormy, Intermittent rainfall indirect fire on Larnes Road at PELICAN CORNER O.33.6 many aircraft over active enemy artillery.
			All guns in Battle except active Sniper at LARNES COPSE

Signed Lt CATCHPOLE
O.C. No 1. M.G.Coy

Army Form C. 2118.

WAR DIARY
or
INTELLIGENCE SUMMARY.
(Erase heading not required.)

Instructions regarding War Diaries and Intelligence Summaries are contained in F. S. Regs., Part II. and the Staff Manual respectively. Title pages will be prepared in manuscript.

Place	Date	Hour	Summary of Events and Information	Remarks and references to Appendices
MARIE FARM	10-12-17 Cont'd		Lt BROWNE & 2/Lt CRAWFORD left night teams relieved the teams in the line - No. 12 was accomplished smoothly without mishap. Enemy fairly even attention to the zone in BYSCHOOTE area.	CW
MARIE FARM	11-12-17		Weather fine - situation very quiet during day. Some shelling at dusk. No two guns at dusk replaced in harassing fire during the night. 2000 rds fired. R.A. guns fired 600 rds at enemy billets	CW
MARIE FARM	12-12-17		Weather fine - situation normal - some shelling at MONDOVI WOOD. Work continued - killed - full force all of night air thing made gas bags casualties 1 O.R. slightly wounded by shrapnel	CW
MARIE FARM	13-12-17		Weather 2/Lt Kirk & 2/Lt ____ gun team - work continued on ____ Barrows Replacements. Harassing fire by 2 guns during the night on enemy cross roads approaches artillery left and roads during neighbourhood of LANES COPSE and ST JANSHOEK ROAD recent enemy attacks.	CW
MARIE FARM	14-12-17		Lt STROVER and 2/Lt BULPITT relieved Lt BROWNE & 2/Lt CRAWFORD in the line Weather cold & fine in the morning. Situation normal during day. Some artillery activity on left during the night.	CW
MARIE FARM	15-12-17		Weather fine - situation normal. Wind continued. Enflilade fire continued on situation normal. Our artillery active. Hostile rifle during the night.	CW
MARIE FARM	16-12-17		Weather fine. 2/Lt CATCHPOLE left and D.M.G.O. 6 reconnoitred our defence line with a view to manned by 2 Company's infantry supplied with 12 guns of F.K. Company in the rear of the defence to by enemy attack all night duty 2/Lt Kirby ____ to the officer on the line. R.E. sub to construct line, blockhouses & shelling in the system	CW
			In firm teams "C" Section Sent by Teams "D" Section. Left to return A/A Stokes in the enemy ____ was sent at dusk ____ Less A.A. Guns fired 2000 rds. Some artillery activity during the night.	CW
MARIE FARM	17-12-17		Lt CATCHPOLE Evacuated to Div. H.Q. to confer with D.M.G.O. respecting the Corps line of defence. Orders first and Evacuated to all officers in the neighbourhood of MONDOVI. Harassing fire during situation quiet. Some shelling in KASSAH road. Hostile aircraft active. Tot R.A. Gun fired at the night by Nos. 3,4,5,6 guns on KASSAH ROAD. dusk	CW
MARIE FARM	18-12-17		Weather hard frost - going on at dawn. Situation during the day quiet. Harassing fire by No. 1,2,3.5 guns. A.A. 6.20 pm many aeroplanes returning by barrage and artillery very accurate. Work continued 2 new positions built.	CW
MARIE FARM	19-12-17		Weather continued frosty - Work continued in the CORPS LINE. Enflilade fire continued - work very difficult owing to hardness of ground. Nos. 2,3,5,6 guns employed in harassing fire during the night. Situation quiet.	CW
MARIE FARM	20-12-17		Lt STROVER & 2/Lt STREETS relieved 2/Lt CARAILE & 2/Lt BULPITT in the line. Situation normal. Enflilade artillery active. Left rifles. Work continued on CORPS LINE and reserve ammunition dumps replenished at CHAMPAUBERT FARM & LES ETRAS. 30,000 rds S.A.A. at ____ dump. G.S.O.1 interviewed Lt COTON Re. Corps Line	CW

(A7883) D. D. & L. London, E.C. Wt. W207/M1672 350,000 4/17 Sch. 53a Forms/C/2118/14

WAR DIARY
or
INTELLIGENCE SUMMARY.
(Erase heading not required.)

Army Form C. 2118.

Instructions regarding War Diaries and Intelligence Summaries are contained in F.S. Regs., Part II. and the Staff Manual respectively. Title pages will be prepared in manuscript.

(Stamp: MACHINE GUN CORPS 219 COY)

Place	Date	Hour	Summary of Events and Information	Remarks and references to Appendices
MARIE FARM	21.12.17		Extract from orders issued by Lt. CATCHPOLE to all officers - Placing formation, 11 CORPS LINE. The Company in conjunction with 2 Companies 14th of the Suffolk Batt. will garrison the Platoon's posts on receipt of "Man from Div. H.Q." The line here forms in turn as the CORPS LINE of RESISTANCE. Guns in the line:-	New orders dated 18.12.17
			Nos 1 & 2 Guns move forward to Battle Positions at U.15.6.90.95 LINES of FIRE given to:	
REF. SHEET BIXSCHOOTE 20 S.W. 1/10,000			" 3 " " " " at U.9.c.6.3 " " at U.9.d.30.35 " " at U.8.d.20.50 " " at U.8.d.70.70 " " at U.8.a.65.60 " " at U.8.a.45.66	All guns - Fixed gun given a defensite Sweeping to Cay on
			Guns at rest:- 2 Guns move forward to new Batt H.Q. at U.9.d. 3.3 " " " N of GOURGI FARM " U.8.a. 9.4 " " " NE of LES LILAS " U.8.c. 3.4 " " " LES LILAS " U.7.a. 7.3	
			New H Guns Mobile { 2 " " to left flank { 2	
			Company H.Q. will be established at CHAMPAUBERT FARM where all messages will be sent.	
			Weather continues frosty - work continued on CORPS LINE mining & shelter. Situation quiet. Nos 3, 4, 5, 6, 7, 8 Guns deployed on Harassing fire from 5.30pm until 7.30am. Targets engaged CORPZY CORNER & PELICAN CORNER approx. point 40,200 Permission obtained to use franchise nearer MARIE FARM & wider Sweep. Lines & Man. the CORPS LINE garden is the task of our engineers.	
MARIE FARM	22.12.17		Weather bright, mild. Relieved in the line from C.C.3-D Sections Aircraft on left when day Active during the daytime. At 4.20pm S.O.S. signal sent up on our right - No development. Post Place 9mm was withdrawn immediately afterwards. Artillery fire opened about 5.15pm. The Bosche replied by us. Corps Line was ... at 7.35 pm. At 9.30 pm Gun Staffs Canvil Rouge Repulse reclaimed it's weapons & returned for about 20 mm. BIXSCHOOTE shelled with 5.9" from 4.15 to 5.20pm. Some direct hits on the road.	
MARIE FARM	23.12.17		Dull day. Some mist. Situation very quiet during day - no aerial activity. Harassing fire during the night on enemy roads. Artillery quiet during night.	
MARIE FARM	24.12.17		Weather cold, misty - Situation quiet throughout day night - no artillery activity. Harassing fire by 4 guns during the night.	
MARIE FARM	25.12.17		Weather generally bright - some stanger. Situation extremely quiet. Xmas dinner for N.C.O's - men later in the day and at rest - Patrolls Night from Company front - Harassing fire by 4 Guns during the night.	
MARIE FARM	26.12.17		Situation normal. Artillery activity, S.O.S. 2112, established. LOS 2115 establishing. Hostile got many little but front family during the night. Gun team stood to throughout. 1.45 am our front artillery activity. Fire by 4 Guns during the night. No development.	
MARIE FARM	27.12.17		Fine - Ground covered with snow. Some shelling at Gun positions during the night. Situation normal. 6 Guns employed on Harassing fire during the night. Enemy aircraft active during day.	

H Cawpole Capt
O.C. 219 Coy

WAR DIARY or INTELLIGENCE SUMMARY

Army Form 2118.

Place	Date	Hour	Summary of Events and Information	Remarks and references to Appendices
MARIE FARM	28-12-17		Weather fine throughout. 4 Teams "A" Sec. & Teams "B" relieved O.D Section in the line. Situation normal. Some shelling near gun positions. 6 Guns engaged harassing fire during the night. Permit will be sent to permit much work. Cpl. HANCOCK returned from leave.	C/6
MARIE FARM	29-12-17		Weather cold, frosty. Situation normal. Intense artillery and trench mortar fire during the neighbourhood of LANNE'S COPSE & OSMETRY Junction. 3 Guns employed on harassing fire.	C/7
MARIE FARM	30-12-17		Weather frosty. Situation quiet. At 4.55 p.m the S.O.S went up on our right. CORPS LINE was immediately manned — no developments. 20 died down at 6.30 p.m.	C/8
MARIE FARM	31-12-17		Weather milder. Situation normal. Work continued on shelters. 4 Guns employed on harassing fire during the night.	C/9

Armond Capt.
O.C. 212 M.G.Coy

1st Division

War Diaries

216th M. G. Corps
Forms part of M.G. BN.

From 1st January To 28 February 1918

WAR DIARY
or
INTELLIGENCE SUMMARY.
(Erase heading not required.)

Army Form C. 2118.

Instructions regarding War Diaries and Intelligence Summaries are contained in F. S. Regs., Part II. and the Staff Manual respectively. Title pages will be prepared in manuscript.

Place	Date	Hour	Summary of Events and Information	Remarks and references to Appendices
MARIE FARM T27 a 7.5	1.1.18		Weather cold. Situation normal. Work on emplacements + shelters continued. 4 guns employed in harassing fire during the night. LT. BROWNE & 2/LT STREETS relieved 2/LT. BURR.PITT + 2/LT CRAWFORD on the line	Cof
REF. SHEET 20 40.030	2.1.18		Weather cold. Situation normal. Work on CORPS LINE continued. Hostile artillery less normal during the day. 4 guns employed in harassing fire.	Cof
MARIE FARM	3.1.18		Weather really cold. 4 Guns. "C" Section relieved Guns of "A" & "B" Section in the line. Situation normal. Hostile aircraft activity owing to bright weather. 4 guns employed in harassing fire during the night.	Cof
MARIE FARM	4.1.18		Weather mild + sunny. Situation very quiet and some enemy aircraft. Ammunition dumps refilled during the evening to guns employed in harassing fire during the evening.	Cof
MARIE FARM	5.1.18		Work continued on CORPS LINE - situation very quiet all guns rested, general clean up ordered D.M.G.O. returned from leave.	Cof
MARIE FARM	6.1.18		Weather warmer. Raining to thaw. Enemy aircraft very active. Hostile artillery shelled LANCIER CROSS ROADS. Relieved 5:30 and 6:30 am. Situation normal.	Cof
MARIE FARM	7.1.18		Weather mild. Situation normal. Preparations for Counter attack work on emplacements + 3 night observation by the Division on our right one gun used on S.O.S. lines at 5.00 am, 1 casualty. LT. STROVER + 2/LT CRAWFORD relieved LT BROWNE + 2/LT STREETS on the line	Cof
MARIE FARM	8.1.18		Surveying party, Laverly Section HQ moved forward to Hill Cover near MONDOVI WOOD. Coy H.Q. on the line at CHAMPAUBERT Situation quiet. Work preparation owing to dark + ground frost.	Cof
MARIE FARM	9.1.18		Capt. HANCOCK took over CHAMPAUBERT FARM as Coy H.Q. in the line 4 guns "A" + "B" Section relieved "C" + "D" Section on the line. Situation normal. 2 hostile air activity ground work quiet.	Cof
MARIE FARM	10.1.18		Weather quiet warmer - 2nd rain. Work continued in CORPS LINE. Situation normal. Hostile artillery more active.	Cof
MARIE FARM	11.1.18		Some rain - ground much softer which enabled work to be carried out more rapidly. Hard work on emplacements + shelters in CORPS LINE. Some hostile artillery activity.	Cof
MARIE FARM	12.1.18		Weather damp. Situation normal. Work on Emplacements and SOS lines at LES LILAS to flank guns of CORPS LINE. Little artillery action. LANCIER CROSS ROADS receiving some attention.	Cof
MARIE FARM	13.1.18		Weather fine. Foggy. Situation normal. Work continued at LES LILAS and CORPS LINE. 2/LT BUR.PITT + 2/LT CARR relieved LT STROVER + 2/LT CRAWFORD in the line.	Cof
MARIE FARM	14.1.18		Weather fine + cold. Lt Colonel LT CATCHPOLE relieved Capt HANCOCK on the line. Situation normal. Work continued.	Cof
MARIE FARM	15.1.18		No other news. Intermittent artillery actions. Work on emplacements + shelters continued.	Ho
MARIE FARM	16.1.18		The Company relief work continued. Heavy rains which hampered relief + caused some little activity in the line. Dugouts at MARIE FM flooded.	Ho

Lt. Amcol Capt O.C. 216 Coy M.G.C.

WAR DIARY or INTELLIGENCE SUMMARY.

Army Form C.2118.

(Erase heading not required.)

Instructions regarding War Diaries and Intelligence Summaries are contained in F. S. Regs., Part II. and the Staff Manual respectively. Title pages will be prepared in manuscript.

Place	Date	Hour	Summary of Events and Information	Remarks and references to Appendices
MARIE FARM	17.1.18		Dugouts at Coy H.Q. rendered untenable, & the rapid rising of water; three accommodation found	
MARIE FARM	18.1.18		2/Lt STREETS relieved 2/Lt CARR in Rught Sector. Heavy Rain. M.B.L flooded. Heavy Rains have swollen the STEENBEEK & BROOMBEEK to flooded swamps, rendered some of them untenable. Pillboxes are flooded to ground level with no means of letting the water out. Roads still flooded - our little dugouts seem still flooded - all men being found at shelter. Situation normal. All influence is rendered practically useless by water – work continued in rear with Infantry.	
MARIE FARM	19.1.18		Weather dull - no rain. Situation normal. Work in influence's continued and taking ammunition. R.E shelter erected 23 in Coy's line	
MARIE FARM	20.1.18		Weather bright, much aerial activity. Left one Enemy. Situation normal. Work continued as previous. Special working party at LES LILAS embarking with a rectangular labelled influence to dugout by Cpl HANCOCK also R.E. party tophibing a pillbox.	
MARIE FARM	22.1.18		Weather dull. Not van G.O.C. inspected the influence at LES LILAS which was satisfied. Colonel Van Straan the Block in the Coy's line at arrangements. Fire made by Capt HANCOCK Situation normal. Quiet aerial activity. Enemy artillery shelling in LR 21US of Trigres "A" & "B" seen. B. Relieved O.B. Section on the line at CATCHABLE FARM.	
MARIE FARM	23.1.18		Weather dull. Situation quiet. Enemy Relief on 49 Regt Reh moved back to CHAMPAUBERT FARM. Box Influence's continue to be in Coy's line by 273 & not until which measure to the whole company regards at right position. Day & night working parties engaged at carrying from the infantry from influence's Completed at MORSTEN R.E. weekly & dig path at dusk & trades by night	
MARIE FARM	24.1.18		Weather fair. Situation very quiet. Work in influence's continued as before all rounds. Carrying hents from infantry dumps all available Enemy gets busy pm during the afternoon. Our Coys night work Company of little artillery shelled our went in carrying infantry.	
MARIE FARM	25.1.18		Weather warm. 2/Lt STOVER relieved 2/Lt BROWNE in the line. Situation normal. Work continued in Coy's line. Some aerial activity	
MARIE FARM	26.1.18		Weather dull & misty. Situation very quiet. No artillery activity owing to misty.	
MARIE FARM	27.1.18		Weather Cold & misty. O.C. 219 M.G. Coy called at H.Q. In conference. Situation normal. Arrangements made for relief of Company by 219 M.G. Coy.	

[signed] O.C. 26 M.G Coy

Army Form C. 2118.

WAR DIARY
or
INTELLIGENCE SUMMARY.
(Erase heading not required.)

Instructions regarding War Diaries and Intelligence Summaries are contained in F. S. Regs., Part II. and the Staff Manual respectively. Title pages will be prepared in manuscript.

Place	Date	Hour	Summary of Events and Information	Remarks and references to Appendices
MARIE FARM	28/1/18		Whole Coy relieved. All guns in the line relieved by 219 M.G.Coy.	
"	29-1-18		Cleaning guns & Kit. Weather fine	
"	30-1-18		Cleaning Equipment, & guns. Weather fine	
"	31-1-18		Commence training, a physical exercises. Weather mild	
			Training continued. Weather cold & misty	

Ernest Galt
O.C. 212 M.G.C.

Army Form C. 2118.

216 M.G. Coy

WAR DIARY
or
INTELLIGENCE SUMMARY.
(Erase heading not required.)

Instructions regarding War Diaries and Intelligence Summaries are contained in F. S. Regs., Part II. and the Staff Manual respectively. Title pages will be prepared in manuscript.

Place	Date	Hour	Summary of Events and Information	Remarks and references to Appendices
MARIE Fm.	FEB 1	9/am	Weather good. Training - Gun Drill, Arms Drill, Gas Drill. Inspection in O/C	AAA
"	2	"	do. Waiting for London Equipment	AAA
"	3	"	do. Parade at hostie aff. Issue of Gun kits & equipment	AAA
"	4	"	do. Arms Drill, Gun Drill. Bell filling, do. Ypres gas Respirator. attn tin 1 to t. Yorker copies team went	AAA
"	5	"	do. Arms Drill. Clancy hunters. aftr. Football	AAA
"	6	"	do. do. aftr.	AAA
"	7	"	Capt. Hancock to Coar Raft Sketch reconnoitre new sector to be taken on 7th. Preparing from r.c. for the line Weather glorious. Capt Hancock, 1st Shorr, "A" Section & details of C+D moved to Montenescourt detrained at ables & Coy HQ. 1st Carr with C Sect. (6 guns) 2/t Shot with D Sect. (5 guns) take over sector & Rin.	AAA
Sugar Camp R.27 a 5.1. (Sheet 58 NW)			Transport. Only Coy. B Sect. 1s Brown reliable. moves to near Transpot Cains Rlwy Crop.	AAA
			H.Q at Sugar Camp	
MORTELDJEST	8	"	REF. MAP. B 10,000. Relief completed. sux guns of No 106 M.G.Coy west relieved, mi at WINCHESTER H.D. one at YORK H.D. Two VAN TIRPITZ Fm. R.YA. 40-40. two at GENOA. R.16. 25.25. LT. CARR in command of 215 M.G.Coy's guns. Four guns of 241 M.G.Coy's views relieved Two at BAVAROISE V.25.c.80.50	

Army Form C. 2118.

WAR DIARY
or
INTELLIGENCE SUMMARY.
(Erase heading not required.)

Instructions regarding War Diaries and Intelligence Summaries are contained in F.S. Regs., Part II. and the Staff Manual respectively. Title pages will be prepared in manuscript.

Place	Date	Hour	Summary of Events and Information	Remarks and references to Appendices
REF MAP ST.JULIEN 1:10000 MOSTELDIE EST C.15.A 90.56	8		Two guns at DELTA Fm. V.19.C.40.10. One gun at PHEASANT TR. V.20.B.15.16. alt. STREETS in command of all M.G. Coy guns. Weather fine	
TURCO Fm REF MAP ST.JULIEN 1:10000 C.15.C.20.25	9		Coy H.Q. move to TURCO Fm. C.15.C.20.50. commence unloading positions on the line. All guns are on British built PillBoxes not hostile, so far. Guns have to be constructed near	#
at TURCO Fm	10		working in Fm in the line. The sector is some quiet. Weather fine	#
CANAL.BK C.25.Q. 50-80	11		Coy H.Q. move to CANAL BANK at C.25.a.50.80. Transport moves to MURAT CAMP B.29.D.50-40. Situation normal. Weather fine	#
	12		Improving camps, waggon lines + gun positions.	#
	13		Lt. KAUFFMANN to take command of "B" Section relieves Lt. Shoults + takes under his command. Lt. STROVER billeted Lt. CARR. & Lt. Evans	
	14		stayed at "B" Sect. with Lt. Twain. Weather wet. Hostile fire – not continued in appreciable. Some small attacks. Situation any quiet.	CCb
	15		Weather Sunny. Situation normal – wet continues a hostile.	CCb
	16		Situation normal, spent Sections in a silence to shelter + Camp where is at CANAL BANK	CCb
	17		weather continues cold sunny. Shells round, wh, expect for all gun position.	CCb

D. D. & L., London, E.C.
(A983.) Wt. W8o7/M1672 350,000 4/17 **Sch. 52a** Forms/C/2118/14

Army Form C. 2118.

WAR DIARY
or
INTELLIGENCE SUMMARY.
(Erase heading not required.)

Instructions regarding War Diaries and Intelligence Summaries are contained in F.S. Regs., Part II. and the Staff Manual respectively. Title pages will be prepared in manuscript.

Place	Date	Hour	Summary of Events and Information	Remarks and references to Appendices
CANAL BANK	18.2.18		Weather fine sunny. Situation normal. Enemy shelling in the vicinity of Von TIRPITZ. Work continued on replacement shelters.	Ref
"	19.2.18		Weather continues fine. Situation on the line. Lifting to rear.	Ref
"	20.2.18		Weather dull. Some rain. Situation normal. Work continued on the line — special shelters work.	Ref
"	21.2.18		Weather fine. Two guns at DELTA HOUSE relieved by No. 1 M.G. Coy. relief reported all correct. Situation normal. Work continued. Enemy own artillery very active, nasty enemy shells.	Ref
"	22.2.18		Weather dull, windy, poor visibility. Situation normal. Capt HANCOCK left to assume 2 battery. Visibility very moderate. Enemy Heavy Artillery bombarded vicinity on our left. BELGIAN Relief — relieved forward unreadable, finished on 9.15 pm	Ref
"	23.2.18		Weather dull — Situation normal. Work continued in the line. Special working parties under Capt. J. HANCOCK preparing latrine positions, shelters etc.	Ref
"	24.2.18		Weather dull — visibility bad. Situation normal. Work continued at battery positions. Artillery activity normal.	Ref
"	25.2.18		Weather fine — Situation normal. Visibility fair. Work in the line continued. Special working parties in Lettres Trenching. Lt STROVER, 2/Lt Relies rel'd. B.12.13. Relies rel'd B.1.B.	Ref
"	26.2.18		C — D Sector, in the line — relief reported correct	
"	26.2.18		Weather fine. Sunny. Situation normal. Work continued in forward area. Artillery activity normal.	Ref
"	27.2.18		Situation normal. Work continued at battery position at Von TIRPITZ No. 2 Artillery in an A/A active from 8 to 9.20 pm — an open emplacement arrived at	Ref
"	28.2.18		Weather showery — some rain. Situation normal. Enemy aircraft very active. Gun shelling on line and Battery position which 2 killed on	Ref

a/– LEFT BATTERY C. Sd. 60.95
RIGHT " C.12.d 20.40 } SHEET 28 N.W. 20,000

Samuel Capt
O.C. 21 May

(A788p) Wt. W8975/M1672 350,000 4/17 D.D. & L., London, E.C. Sch. 52a. Forms/C/2118/14